Journey Across CHINA

Journey Across
CHINA

Photography by
Charles E. Brooks

ORANGE FRAZER PRESS
Wilmington, Ohio

ISBN: 1-882203-95-X

Additional copies of *Journey Across China* may be ordered directly from:

Charles E. Brooks	or	Orange Frazer Press
BROOKS Photography		Box 214
214 E. Eighth Street		Wilmington, Ohio 45177
Cincinnati, Ohio 45202		www.orangefrazer.com
brooksphotog@aol.com		1.800.852.9332
513.369.0031		

Prints of photos from *Journey Across China* may be purchased from:
Charles E. Brooks
BROOKS Photography
214 E. Eighth Street
Cincinnati, Ohio 45202
brooksphotog@aol.com
513.369.0031

Designed by Danielle Chen
Printed in China

Library of Congress Cataloging-in-Publication Data

Brooks, Charles E., 1946-
    Journey across China / photography by Charles E. Brooks.
        p. cm.
    ISBN 1-882203-95-X
    1. Brooks,Charles E., 1946---Journeys--China--Pictorial works. 2.china-Pictorial
works. I. Title

DS712.B77 2003
951--dc21   2002193193

Preface

I first visited China in April 2001, commuting through Hong Kong and taking the train to industrial Guangzhou (Canton) 85 miles north. As a Westerner, I was culturally shocked. As a photographer, I was fascinated. I had never seen anything of such human scale.

There are over 1.25 billion people living in China today. China is a very diverse country with city populations in the multi-millions. Most Westerners do not even know some of these cities exist. Cities that, in spite of their great size, still have their own unique character.

This culture has been diverse and changing as a civilization for over 5,000 years.

Rural China exhibits as much diversity from one area to another as the cities do. From Mount Everest in the Himalayans, to the Gobi Desert in the North, to the more wet and semi-tropical South, China wears many different landscapes and regional cultures. To truly experience China, I had to see much more than Guangzhou.

In May 2002, I returned with my Hasselblad to photograph as much as I could of this curious country. The journey began in Beijing, the modern capital of China. I traveled 1,700 miles West to Lhasa, Tibet by way of Xian, the ancient capital, and Chengdu, the home of the giant panda.

From Tibet, we headed East again to Chongqing where I boarded a Yangtze River cruise for an amazing 520 miles to Wuhan. This was timely, because the Three Gorges Dam, now under construction, will be completed soon and much of the river will be flooded over the next few years. Estimates are that more than 1.5 million people will have to be relocated. Whole cities are being moved up the banks to higher ground. There are images in this book that by 2009 will be under water.

The final destination of the journey was Shanghai, on the coast about 420 miles East of Wuhan. Shanghai has been a trading port for hundreds of years. The Chinese there are accustomed to Westerners, especially the French and British.

If there was one generalization to make about China, it might be that China is changing. In fact, this culture has been diverse and changing as a civilization for over 5,000 years. Today, the pace of change is likely faster than anytime in history. The result is a stark contrast between the old and the new. The images in this book reveal both sides in the landscape, cities, and the people.

From Beijing to Lhasa to Shanghai, across 3,500 miles, this is my photographic story *Journey Across China*.

Charlie Brooks, BROOKS Photography

Beijing

BEIJING (PREVIOUSLY PEKING) IS THE MODERN CAPITAL OF CHINA. BY 1260, KUBLAI KHAN, GRANDSON OF GENGHIS KHAN, REBUILT THE CITY AS DADU AND MOVED HIS CAPITAL HERE. UNDER THE MING DYNASTY (1368–1644), THE CAPITAL SHIFTED TO

Nanjing (the Southern Capital) before returning in the 15th century, to the newly renamed Beijing (Northern Capital).

Today, Beijing is a modern city of 13.8 million people. It is rapidly growing with new high-rise office and residential construction. Beijing is preparing for the 2008 Summer Olympic Games, constructing several huge arenas. Westerners are not commonplace here. "Beijingers" often stared, and looked for every opportunity to say "hello.

My photographs primarily illustrate the ancient side of Beijing (the

Forbidden City, the Summer Palace). The Forbidden City is so named because it was out of bounds to common people for 500 years. Surrounded by a moat and wall, it comprised the imperial residence for the emperor and his family. Entering from the south through the Gate of Supreme Harmony, across from Tiananmen Square is an enormous portrait of Mao Zedong.

Other images in Beijing include the back streets where people still live clustered in Hutongs. On the north side of the Forbidden City is the Summer Palace and Prospect Hill (Jingshan), the highest point in old Beijing. The image of the Palace in the valley is taken from this point. The hill owes its height to the earth hauled from the excavating of the moat system surrounding the Forbidden City.

About 50 miles north of Beijing, is a restored section of the Great Wall. The photographs were taken on the steepest side of the wall in Badaling Pass. The Great Wall is over 2,500 years old, and stretches for over 3,000 miles. Over a million Chinese built the wall, and many died doing so. It was a humbling experience.

The Ming Tombs are south of the Great Wall on the way back to Beijing. In 1407, the emperor Yongle sought a burial place of "gentle winds and winding waters." Since Yongle, all but one of the Ming emperors have been buried here. The Sacred Way to the tombs begins at a great marble gateway, followed by the Avenue of Animals. This walkway is lined with stone statues of real and mythical beasts leading to the tombs. The statues alternate standing and kneeling. At night, the statues switch!

Xian

XIAN, PRONOUNCED "SHEE AHN," IS LOCATED IN THE SHAANXI PROVINCE. XIAN IS THE ANCIENT CAPITAL OF CHINA. IN 221 B.C., CHINA'S FIRST EMPEROR, QIN SHI HUANG, UNITED CHINA AND PROCLAIMED XIAN AS ITS CAPITAL. AS PART OF THE UNIFICATION,

he joined "state" walls to form the Great Wall. The Qin (pronounced chin) Dynasty lasted only from 221 to 206 B.C.

The Han Dynasty followed (206 B.C.–220 A.D.) expanding prosperity and continuing to reside in Xian as their Capital. Both of China's first dynasties took advantage of the natural defenses of the Huang (Yellow) River to the east and the Qin Ling Mountains to the south.

In 1974, local farmers digging a well inadvertently discovered the Qin Army Vaults. They are known broadly, today, as the terracotta warriors.

The terracotta warriors were distributed over three large underground platforms. A Fourth pit was discovered in 1978, and two bronze chariots with four horses in 1980. There are estimated to be more than 7,000 warriors with four main categories of figures: chariot warriors,

infantrymen, cavalrymen, and horses. There are generals, middle ranking officers, lower ranking officers, ordinary soldiers, armored warriors, and kneeling warriors. Considered to be the archaeological discovery of the century, this excavation is spiritually moving.

During the Tang Dynasty (618–908), it was the Silk Road trade that made the ancient city rich and prosperous. Buddhism had long developed along the Silk Road since the Han Dynasty. In Xian, the Wild Goose Pagoda was added to the Temple of Great Mercy and Goodness around 650 A.D. This is where the monk, Xuan Zang, brought Buddhist manuscripts from India to be translated into Chinese.

Calligraphy is set into the walls on both sides of the pagoda. Locals and pilgrims from other parts of China come here to light candles and pray for a happy life.

The Tang Dynasty Cultural Show in Xian has the Wild Goose Pagoda painted on the backdrop behind the dancers. The color and grace of China's theatrical presentations are moving. The photo I selected is only one representative view.

Xian has an ancient city wall built during the Ming Dynasty (1368–1644). Its rectangular perimeter is nearly 8 miles long. Ceremonial gateways and watchtowers are in place at the four points of the compass. Walking the Ming Wall is great for photography, site seeing, and people watching.

Chengdu

CHENGDU HAD BEEN THE ECONOMIC AND CULTURAL CENTER OF THE SICHUAN BASIN FOR MORE THAN 2,000 YEARS. THROUGHOUT THE HAN DYNASTY, CHENGDU'S COMMERCE WAS IN LACQUER WARE, GOLD AND SILVER HANDICRAFTS, AND BROCADE PRODUCTION.

When the Han Dynasty collapsed, the prominence of Chengdu also ended.

Most of Chengdu's ancient walls have been destroyed, making way for modern office and apartment buildings. Chengdu is proud of their flower gardens and parks throughout the city. The revival of Chendu has reinstated its reputation as "the City of Hibiscus."

Today, a three-story high statue of Chairman Mao Zedong stands in front of the city's exhibition center. The park, across the street, is neatly landscaped. Park patrollers keep visitors from walking or sitting on the grass. Littering is out of the question!

Chendu is also known as the "Land of Abundance" because of its ancient marketplace. Fresh fruits, vegetables, and any number of exotic delicacies can be found in this historic commercial area. The marketplace, itself, continues to shrink as its borders are leveled for new construction.

As a result of the revival, the contrast between the old and the new is dramatic in Chengdu. While the long ride from the airport reveals miles upon miles of rural poverty, the downtown is exploding with commercial development.

Nevertheless, wander a block or two behind the modern marvels. Duck into an alley and discover the disappearing historic neighborhoods. Here you will see old men on three-wheelers making their way through the marketplace. Shoulder boards make carrying loads easy by hanging baskets of goods from each end.

My photographs of Chengdu are exclusively of the old town. What may appear as an alley is actually the walkway to someone's home. The family vehicle, usually a bike, is parked just outside the front door. Children play on the family cart, perhaps what we might consider as the family van. Colorful rag mops stored by the door present an image of still life in another world's gallery.

I came to Chengdu to photograph the giant pandas. I found them sleeping in trees, and munching on sugar cane. The cubs were playing what looked like a game of "hit and run." While they appear playful and cuddly, they are still bears!

I enjoyed photographing the people, bikes, and bears of Chengdu, another city of millions, but, again, very unlike ancient Xian, and very unlike the center of government, Beijing. But if you are seeking cultural diversity within China, you must see Tibet!

Lhasa

LHASA IS THE CAPITAL OF TIBET. A CITY OF JUST OVER 100,000 PEOPLE, AND JUST ABOUT 12,000 FEET ABOVE SEA LEVEL, LHASA IS THE HOME OF "LAMAISM", A LOCAL ADAPTATION OF BUDDHISM. IN 1573, THE FOUNDER OF THE "YELLOW HAT" BECAME THE FIRST DALAI LAMA.

Rising from the top of Red Hill (the only hill within Lhasa) is the home and resting place for all but one of the Dalai Lamas, the Potala Palace. The original Potala Palace was built in the 7th century as a place for meditation by King Songtsen Gampo. The current structure was built in the 17th century. It is a treasure trove of many priceless antiques, hand-written scriptures, and the mausoleum for the Dalai Lamas. The golden Stupas are onion shaped pagodas that contain the Dalai Lama embalmed in a sitting position.

The Potala Palace is 13 stories and more than 1,000 rooms. Today, the palace is no longer the home of the Dalai Lama. The Dalai Lama is considered an exiled government. Religion, however, is recognized in China, and religious pilgrims come to the Potala Palace and other temples to pray. Monks maintain the palace. My favorite photo in the book is called "Windowlight". It was taken in the hall next to the Dalai Lama's bedchamber. The wall painting glows with the setting sun.

Nearby, at the Sera Monastery, monks still gather in their bright, red robes every afternoon to discuss and debate the fine points of Buddhism. One standing monk asks the question. One sitting monk answers the question. If they agree, the standing monk slaps his fist into his other palm. If not, the debate rages on.

Tibetans (many are nomads from the mountains) come to Lhasa for their annual religious pilgrimage. Prayer flags flapping in the wind keep the evil spirits away from homes and property. Prayer Wheels provide the same protection while spinning. Many temples have drum-like wheels throughout. You can find them all around the perimeter of the Potala Palace. Additionally, pilgrims carry hand-held wheels with prayer notes inside. They constantly are spinning them as they walk to the temple.

The Jokhang Temple is one of

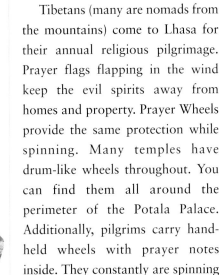

Tibet's holiest shrines, built in 647 A.D. Just as the Potala Palace, the temple was built in celebration of King Songtsen Gampo's marriage to Princess Wencheng. The Jokhang is the spiritual center of Tibet. Pilgrams lie prostrate outside its walls in prayer. Eventually, they crowd into the temple, lighting candles and sitting in meditation. The interior of the temple is dark and filled with the essence of burning Yak butter (fat). Better to go to the roof to take in the exterior gold leaf, views, and ceremonial horns. A great view of the Potala Palace can be seen from the rooftop.

Outside the Jokhang, is the Barkhor market where storekeepers virtually grab you to see their wares. The market is also full of beggars who are pros! After photographing a woman with a baby on her back, I gave her a couple quan for her cooperation. Mistake! I had to finally duck into a restaurant to get away from the resulting crowd. Sometimes, what is culturally interesting is not what you see, but what you do not see. In Tibet, do not expect to see cemeteries. Few Tibetans are buried in stupas or graves of any variety. Typically, one has a choice: a sky burial, or a water burial. The sky burial consists of an above ground bed on pillars, usually on a hilltop. Over time, the birds pick away the body. Eventually, the remains are gone to the sky!

The disappearance of the remains in a water burial is somewhat more immediate. The remains are chopped into pieces on the riverbank and cast into the water. Fish and current take care of the rest.

Peace be with you.

The Yangtze River

THE CITY OF CHONGQING, A BEAUTIFUL MOUNTAIN CITY, IS WHERE I BOARDED THE VICTORIA II FOR THE CRUISE DOWN THE YANGTZE RIVER. CHONGQING CLAIMS TO BE THE LARGEST POPULATED AREA IN CHINA—OVER 30 MILLION PEOPLE. THIS FIGURE

might go well beyond what most would consider to be city limits. The city is so hilly that bicycles are not prevalent as in many other cities in China.

It was important to photograph the banks and valleys of the Yangtze (an ancient trade route where a third of the population of China still live), because by 2009, much of the river will be flooded due to the completion of the Three Gorges Dam. Over the centuries, the Yangtze has flooded in the spring costing many lives and laying waste to river fields and towns.

The Three Gorges Dam will allow for flood control and stable economic growth for the river valley. Over the 520-mile cruise from Chongqing to Wuhan, it is estimated that 1.5 million people will have to be relocated. Many towns, today, will be entirely

under water over the next few years. Cities are being rebuilt on higher ground, and their current structures destroyed to prevent them from becoming navigational hazards.

Fengdu is one such city. High above Fengdu is the "Ghost City" with numerous temples housing silent ghosts and devils. While the lower Fengdu will be under water, Ghost City will remain dry.

The vertical cliffs of the gorges are pocketed with ancient, square holes likely used to suspend walkways for ancient civilizations. High on the cliffs, there still remain wooden coffins, some hundreds of years old. China is doing all it can to preserve the artifacts and temples before the flooding.

River traffic remains heavy. Commercial barges and tourist cruisers are busy on the river all year around. The photo of the

dragon boat on the cover is a Chinese tourist cruise boat. The majority of tourists in China are Chinese.

The three gorges, Qutang, Wu, and Xiling are dramatic. Also, an area called the Three Lesser Gorges (Dragon Gate, Misty, and Emerald) is perpetually shrouded in misty clouds. Add the start of the rainy season, and you have dramatic light and imagery!

The construction of the Three Gorges Dam is an engineering wonder. When completed, it will be the largest dam in the world raising the level of the Yangtze River 150 feet or more. The dam will provide for 10,000-ton ocean-going cargo ships and cruise liners to navigate the 1,500 miles inland from the Pacific to the port city of Chongqing.

Shanghai

As a city, Shanghai is considered to be the largest in China with over 14 million people. Shanghai is Chinese for "on the sea." It is situated on the Huangpu River, near the Yangtze's mouth to the East China Sea.

Shanghai is China's most important port, commercial hub, and industrial center. It has been a trade center for centuries. As a result, Westerners are somewhat commonplace here. The French and British have taken residence here for years. While Shanghai has been called the "Paris of the East," I think of it as similar to Singapore.

Little remains of the Old Town. What is there appears to be very commercialized. Shops, restaurants, and Tea Houses are what you will find there. Of more beauty and significance, however, are the Yu Yuan Gardens. Here, I found beauty in the viewfinder! The dragon undulating along the top of the garden walls provided dramatic impact.

What the Old Town lacked in historical value, it overcame with color! Fire red lanterns and brightly colored flags made the walk worthwhile. Outside of the Old Town walls are older, more typical neighborhoods. The image of the old woman and man at the watermelon stand is a good example of this. Bicycles and cars compete with one another for position. Pedestrians, bicycles, and autos all have the same rights. Watch yourself! It is a free-for-all out there.

Maybe I did not find the right neighborhoods. I did not find the opium houses, cockfights, or dens of sin. Nor was I kidnapped and pressed into service on a freighter. Even the Bund, the famous waterfront promenade, provided a skyline of ultra modern commercial buildings on the opposite bank. No sampans, no junks were in sight.

What I did see was commerce and color! Shanghai is shopping. The walk down Shanghai's Nanjing Road was exceptionally colorful. Pedestrians crossed intersections via walking bridges, which provided great camera vantage points for the photographer. The street seemed to go for several straight miles, packed side to side with busy shoppers.

Shanghai was easy. Taxis were very inexpensive. Traveling across town might cost only $1.50 in U.S. currency. Cultural shows, including acrobats and dancers, are spectacular. Shanghai is a great transitional city before coming home to the Western life. Shanghai was another great city with its own unique character. It was a fitting close to photography and a *Journey Across China*.

ABOUT THE IMAGES

Cover Chinese excursion boats cruise the Yangtze River. Today, most of the tourists in China are Chinese. Foreign tourism, however, is growing. No longer must one have a "sponsor" to secure a travel visa in China.

BEIJING

page 8 In Tiananmen Square, a vendor leaves his bike to work the crowd on foot. The "front door" to the Forbidden City, Gate of Heavenly Peace, dominates the background. A portrait of Chairman Mao greets those who enter.

page 9 Many businesses who employ a large staff, begin each day with a street formation. Here, the instructions of the day are conveyed. Hotels and restaurants are very efficient. Everyone has a role, even if it is to watch the hallway (for security or assistance).

page 10 While modern Beijing is exploding with new high-rise construction; there are still remnants of "old" Beijing. Here, a bakery.

page 11 The Emperor's Summer Palace has many beautiful gardens, walls, and buildings. This is typical roof and wall construction.

page 12 The Chinese enjoy touring Beihai Park and cannot resist waving to the Westerners.

page 13 View from Prospect Hill (Jingshan), the highest point in Beijing. The hill owes its height to the earth hauled from the excavating of the moat system surrounding the Forbidden City.

page 14 The old streets of Beijing can be chaotic to Westerners. Many royal estates were converted to multi-family dwellings (Hutongs) after 1949.

page 15 A bride and groom wait their turn to be photographed in the park across the street from the photographer's studio.

page 16 Typical Chinese sculpture in the Forbidden City consists of lions and dragons in granite detail.

page 17 Interior of the Forbidden City. As the emperor's residence, the Forbidden City was off limits to all but the family and staff for over 500 years.

page 18 Pilgrims often come to the Forbidden City to pray.

page 19 Parts of the Forbidden City are used by the military for training.

page 20 The walls of the Forbidden City are over 600 years old.

page 21 The Golden Water Stream flows through the Forbidden City under four sacred bridges.

page 22 One of the sacred bridges over the Golden Water Stream. Pilgrims cross over the bridge on their way to the Gate of Supreme Harmony.

page 23 Walk along the Imperial Garden in the Forbidden City.

page 24 The Golden Water Stream in the Forbidden City.

page 25 For many, the walls of the Forbidden City provide a place to rest, and think.

LHASA

THE YANGTZE RIVER

page 82 | The Yangtze River stretches for 1,500 miles from the Pacific to the port city of Chongqing.

page 83, 84 & 85 | Sanpans are as common as ocean freighters on the Yangtze. One third of China's population lives and works on the Yangtze.

page 86 | Vertical cliffs of the gorges are pocketed with ancient, square holes used to suspend walkways for ancient civilizations.

page 87 | Kites in the sky.

page 88 | Fengdu will be entirely under water by 2009.

page 89 | The Chinese garden in Wuhan on the Yangtze.

page 90 | The streets of Wuhan.

SHANGHAI

page 92 | Shanghai's Nanjing Road is shopping and color.

page 93 | Mother and daughter in Shanghai's shopping district.

page 94 | Old Town in Shanghai. A district that appeals to tourists.

page 95 | Just outside of Old Town is old Shanghai, where the locals conduct their commerce.

page 96 | The color of old Shanghai.

page 97 | Watermelon wagon on the streets of Shanghai.

page 98 | Yu Yuan Gardens in the center of Old Town Shanghai.

ABOUT THE AUTHOR

I developed my love for photography in the 1960's as a teenager. My father, who was a studio photographer in the early 1940s, had given me my first camera, an Argus C44 rangefinder. What a technological advance that camera was! Its external light meter was almost as big as the lens. Since then, I have improved my equipment locker considerably, both in format and technology.

What hasn't changed is how I feel about the art of creating images. I think every successful photographer takes hundreds of mental photographs everyday with their own eyes. When you routinely visualize everything you see in terms of composition and light, you cannot help but develop a passion for learning how to turn your vision into a print that others can enjoy. You want others to see what you see. Share the experience.

So, after high school, I went on to earn my BA at Ohio State, graduating in 1968. By 1972, I managed to complete my military obligation and my MBA in marketing. But, something came up. I had an offer to work for Procter & Gamble, and couldn't refuse.

It's ok, I still continued with photography; occasionally shooting weddings, and building family albums that would embarrass our national archives in Washington, D.C. Before I realized it, I was approaching 30 years with P&G, having traveled literally around the globe. I was in a position to bring my P&G career to a successful close in 2001.

At last, I was free to expand BROOKS Photography, founded in 1999, into a full-time second career. By May 2002, I had begun my Journey Across China. I hope you will enjoy the journey as much as I.

Charlie Brooks

P.S. Yes, I still have the Argus C-44 in my closet.